WITH NO SWEAT AT ALL

Alisa Velaj

Translated from the Albanian by Ukë Zenel Buçpapaj

Červená Barva Press
Somerville, Massachusetts

Červená Barva Press
P.O. Box 440357
W. Somerville, MA 02144-3222

www.cervenabarvapress.com
Bookstore: www.thelostbookshelf.com

Cover art: *Woman Before the Rising Sun*
Caspar David Friedrich (Circa 1818)

Cover design: William J. Kelle
Production: Steve Asmussen

ISBN: 978-1- 950063-46-8
Library of Congress Control Number: 2021942505

CONTENTS

WITH NO SWEAT AT ALL

The Foundations Have Remained Open

THE HOUSE

The house, which is about to collapse, belongs to you,
And the trees, which the storm fell last night,
Belonged to your yard.
Let me contour your dimensions
In another space,
Where the roof timbers are much more secure,
Where the roots have stuck
Into firm ground:
Only then I can embrace you without fearing anything…

THE UNDERGROUND

No dusk sound
Succeeds in scratching silence.
No door creak
Succeed in foreboding anything inside me.
I hide under your chest
As if I were a seagull wounded
By roaring winds
That would drive even the fool crazy:
I am a Bohemian
Fearing I might lose things
That never belonged to me…

FULLY AWARE

Your insecurity makes me lose my head,
For winds have always bended trees,
And cuckoos have always screamed on branches,
Yet leaves never translated into flocks of ravens…

PINKS

Pinks
Living a lonely life in glass vases.
My sleepy being
Breathing on the pillow.
'Pinks are blood,
They are red blood,' I say to you…

THE FOUNDATIONS HAVE REMAINED OPEN

The leaf fell again
In the same place.
It is the raked soil
They tilled with a harrow last night.
The foundations have remained open,
Sheltering a few stones
Fallen from nowhere,
Which opened another furrow
In my memory…

THE JUVENILE SONG

The child murmured an obscure song,
Waiting for the snail to walk out of its shell.
High firs standing near one another like skull bones do
Set up the fence surrounding him…

A Tiny Palm Branch

To my uncle Pelasgus

Out of all the flowers that had covered your exhausted body
Only a tiny palm branch has remained
Your shoulders could not hold all the greenery
Something had to be left hovering in the sad sky
Of this September day
Something resembling the aroma of flowers and the nostalgia of blue colours
The tiny palm branch had to be forgotten
In a corner of a room
For they had pulled it from the Life Tree against its will
As if to tell me
That I loved you more than the words
For the earthly roots of loves as pure as you
Are quite fragile…

Threshold

To Mario

The child builds a house inside the house
A small hut of bed pillows
A little lamp lights the tiny shelter
The child reads about midgets with his mouth open
And feels happy to have a tiny house like theirs
Whereas Cinderella sings songs
And prepares sweets for the child and his friends coming from the fairytale
Outside a stormy rain falls the last leaves of trees
And the wind howls like a crazy bitch with no reason at all
Sometimes his mother sings to deceive the stormy rain
With melodies sweeter than all the songs
Ever heard going on between Scylla and Charybdis
Tonight Odysseus will certainly invent an Ithaca in Orpheus' arms
Sleepy though…

Five Views of Mists

1

The blind sees
With the eyes of mists

2

Even trees hide their greenery
In mists

3

The sun buried in mists
Looks like a pale moon
And the river's memory is
The bluish green oblivion of pearls

4

Cities and mists write
The chronicles of the sun's solitude

5

Mists even without solitude inside
Count almost nothing…

PILLOWS OF SOUNDS

What more do you seek from sunsets, man?
A bunch of copper leaves
Fell on the strings of the guitar leaning against the tree trunk
And slept the most anxious sleep
Using sounds as pillows
The solitude of seas persecutes the leaves in dreams
Like the shadows of seasons do to man
What more do you seek from sunsets
You being that keep travelling on the shores of oblivion?
The guitar will always succeed
In weaving serenades
An inexistent bridge can connect no river banks
Be a sunrise if you want to understand the sunsets, man
Someone called the Caspian Lake a 'Sea'
And to this day they write it so on every world map…

THERE WHERE I DANCE

My house is
There where I dance

The wind's shadow dances through trees
It dances to me
It dances to you

My temple is
There where I keep quiet and pray

The wind's shadow implores
A leaf's mercy

(Thousands of onlookers walk in city streets
Without knowing why they cry
Without knowing why they laugh)

My repentance is
There where I implore love

The autumn's embers
Burn the shadows to ashes...

WAITING FOR THE WINTER

Waiting for the winter
I feel the breath of the lands that have caught cold
Just because of thinking that cold weather will soon launch the assault
Just because of thinking that frost is on its way to them
The anxiety of leaves saddens me as well
(My loves rustle with anxiety)
But why should loves and lands blame us
For their making haste to reach solitude
Holding torches in their hands?
Why should our vague memory that fails to remember
When the first sunset hit it
Throw blame on us?

CURIOSITY UNDER A NAKED MOON

Naked songs
Under a naked moon
My curiosity defeats paleness
And tries to keep quiet as long as possible
Look at the boreal nights for a short while, darling
Something worthier than nothingness
Must necessarily be hiding
Beyond my curiosity and the lethargic mornings
The frightened sparrows of your breath
Are the first accords of the guitar lost
Somewhere under the snow or amidst the moon's bones
No one knows
Where other accords and other solitudes
Come from or go to
Come into being, die again, and live three other lives, honey
Just to bring curiosity back to life for a short while…

MOZART APPEARED ON THE STAGE

They all said that
There was the place where acacia flowers take their rest
They all said that
And a child pointed to Salieri's grave
Lying a little further ahead
At dusk when oblivion invades the rivers
Mozart appeared on stage holding acacia flowers in his hands
And wept…

SHE

She is calmer than her songs
She falls asleep watching the twisted veins of trees
She is luckier than night and darkness
Blood capillaries will set fire to her moon
And night and darkness will run on all fours fearing her and her moon.

THE CAW

Crows' caws
Piercing the air through
In the northern sky…

The beloved winter
Is a season to spend …

It's cold air
Sticks in your throat
Because of slaughtered birds …

Unknown Matters

Moonbeams of suicide effect
On drunkard walking on the hidden streets
Of a city buried in darkness.

The full moon,
Next to his house
(Where a neon light has grown pale),
Interweaves troubled thoughts
About unknown matters,
Which, accidentally (or out of ill will),
They baptized with real names.

The Call of the Wolves

I have now come
With my peaceful soul and breath
Don't expect to single out anything at first sight
Only on Sundays soul is a contemplating view
Breath stays hovering between me and the world

I shall stay a little longer, and then I shall leave
Otherwise the ripen apples will rot with gloom

I shall stay as long as needed, not a single moment more
Departure becomes meaningful when the sun's winds blow
Arrival is blessed with a few rain drops
On a day as clear as the Ionian Sea waters

Don't implore me at all to stay this Monday
The blue of the waters is the voice of my journeys
The blessed call of the depth of the skies
The only happiness empty of farewell sadness

THE HYMN OF MADNESS

The old women witch river banks
Wetting white sheets of snow
And wrapping dead mouse in them

God forgive them
They do not know what they are doing

The sheets belonged to a virgin girl
They killed the mouse in a dark hole at night
(Girls and mouse are their sacrifice)

God forgive them
They know no other light

They begin to sing such a luring melody
Under the rhythm of steps that has lost the way home
Without knowing that the river has no memory at all
It knows only how to flow and flow, only this much...

My God, I shall not speak any more
From today on the muteness of the ocean will be my language

THE SUNSET AND THE LUMPS

Of what was it I was thinking?
So the meaning escapes.

An excerpt from *Metaphors of a Magnifico* by Wallace Stevens

The first man said that the sunset was visiting the city
Together with one or two lumps
The second man said that the lumps had arrived at sunset
The third man spent one full day thinking only about the lumps
Then he spent a full winter night thinking only about the sunsets
Afterwards he thought about both the sunsets and the lumps
At the end he concluded that the first two men were wrong
He also denied to have thought about them…

A Gospel of Light

For my mother

Mom, don't let the autumn leaves
Fly over your head
They contain sorrows of birds
And whispers of breezes and memories of desert winds
Raising clouds of reddish dust
(Its colour is that of autumn leaves)

Mom, this sea morning is so bright
That every ray of sunshine entangled with your hair
Tells me that there are whites whiter than the snow
Heights higher than the sky
And that it is never late to learn the language of love

This sky of gulls is so peaceful
That your deep eyes, these two tiny blue holes
Can hide the purest Gospel of light
That leaves and winds read once in a while...

THE CRICKET AND THE MOON

The cricket sings to the night and the moon
The moon is full and yellow

Sometimes the cricket does not sing to the moon
She stays hidden among the clouds and shines on its self

The cricket continues singing at moonless nights
Thus falling a prey to predators

But even when the moon appears in the sky, the same happens
The predator may devour the cricket together with its song

A Duet With Two Solos

I cannot stop time
Moreover, I cannot stop
Thinking either
Thinking in time
Time of thinking
It is exactly as if trying to outline
Within everything
The borders of nothingness of reddish colour
More or less like that of the autumn leaves

Then there comes the winter
That is not enough for itself
Let alone for the sparrows

Spring is the season that always
Approaches to its end
Seeing off saps of desires
Riding two white pigeons
On a tree branch under the scorching sun

Everything is worthless
Even stopping of breath
Is a time hiding whims of desires
In a sea as deep as Orpheus's pains

Agaves

"There are so many dawns which have not yet shed their light."
Indian Maxim

One morning
Agaves appeared to me
Wandering barefooted
On dry rocks of Colorado

My patience suffocating
With my aching soles
Made me stop to rest for a while
And suddenly agaves appeared to me
With their petals turned towards the sun

Since then I have learned to measure time
With shadows of flowers
And walk freely on horizons
Of dawns which have not yet shed their light…

A Tale

Once upon a time, sunflowers grew
Far from you,
With their face always turned
Towards God.

At this gloomy night
When crickets sing hymns to sadness,
I am telling about these temples of light
To you who loved lilies and daises,
Burning with the same ardent fire.

I am telling it to you,
My love coming the homeland of waves,
And even dying strange deaths…

HITTING

Scream
As much as you can,
Chewing on my bone.

Scream
As much as you can,
Exploring my chest.

Then, at dusk, drown your scream
In the waters of this sea.

I will calm down if you make my soul hit me
With the taste of scream
Visiting my palate and tongue...

CANDLES

On my shoulders, I carry skies colder than yours,
As well as many candles lit
To cakes I lost in a place I cannot remember.

Tonight, you tell me to remain silent,
Watch the stars give their performance,
And see them fall,
Feeling as hungry as I did once
When I anxiously expected
The waves to foam.

But now the candles have melted in my hands,
And I don't know where to put their remains…

A Saga

At sunset
The ivory shore
Changed into a bay and a season of firs

There I have met both water and fire

Wind sounds
Fell fearfully on leaves
And became birds

Then at the end of winter
The fire sailed
Towards another bay
And the birds
Fled from the greenery

Then bending my body down
I watched the corals
And blessed the fir
With its face turned towards the East…

You Would Have Been An Uninvited Guest, Ares

The thought that I had lost you
Appeared to me in a dream tonight, Ares
A flame struggled to devour
A crucified Christ
And I, horrified, in a roofless room
Protected myself from the bats running into the walls

Ares, my sadness was so deep
That I woke up from the dream with much haste
Outside the roof tiles flew with the wind
And the bats lay dead in the yard
Like Pyrrhus' soldiers after the battle…

It was better that you did not appear in that horrible mess
You would have been an uninvited guest, Ares…

THERE WILL COME A NIGHT

Never force yourself into singing songs
Let the sounds find the path leading to you

For there will come a time
A time will come
When the ghosts of the hallow tree
On which you are building your house
Will conquer your forest, your yard, your being
As if they were metastasis of darkness
Invading a church that has never been a church

Never trust the song
For the cuckoo often hides itself in the nightingale's voice
The nightingale, yes, the nightingale is always the nightingale
Train your ears so that the sounds cannot deceive you

For there will come a night
A night will come
When the heart of the hallow tree
Will be our final home

Then every morning the nightingales will migrate never to return
And you will remain a cuckoo sharing company with the blind night

ALEPH

It's late, it's too late
To drown in the greenery of the forest
And the birds of oblivion have long ran away
With their chirps still hanging on branches…

It's late, it's too late
To celebrate rebirths under shades of firs
The branches now belong solely to the forests
The forests belong to themselves and the chirps

It's late
It's too late
The grass had warned you

The Feast

Holding a glass of water in its hands
Myself, the colour of chocolate
Performs the rites of sadness

A white homeland
Stuck in its throat

THE SONG OF A LITTLE GIRL FROM ACRE

I do not know if one day I shall become a poetess
In my home city I have never felt the anxiety of cold weather
Or autumn's arrivals or skies loaded with clouds
Wetting the roof of my house

I lack so many things I need to become a poets
At hot nights mosquitoes redden my body
These cursed beings cover my body in swollen spots
They are so big that I fear people will see them despite my dress

In the morning I wake up early with my soul singing songs
At night I see lakes and seas and oceans in my dreams
So walking to school along streets without pavements
I close my eyes as if I were a swan or a gull
There I feel the bite of some other mosquito
Coming from the swamp on the left of the street...

I again I cry for I fear one day I shall not become a poetess
For I lack so many things
I lack the leaves, the rains, and the seasons
I lack everything that is free and beautiful

I am an only daughter of the season o palms
And a distant cousin of the desert cactus
I wear thorns to protect my water from evaporating
For everyday I water my sadness
With lakes, with seas, and with oceans...

The Incense

I again pray after silence and stay silent after prayer.
The lily of my dreams has long fled the white colour.
The white of snows, the white of petals… and even
the white of eggs.
The raven, blacker than death, haunts the lily,
fading away on the wings of storms.

ETERNITY

Striking against stones, even ice
Crumbled into countless crystal chips.

Mythic stubbornness
With Sisyphus' lymph in bones
Always swims in cold sweat.

Might Helios' chariot have passed by here?

Anti-Narcissus

Rebelling
Often fits
With a profligate lad
My cactus flower!

None allowed
The theft of elixir
Furiously rolled
Down scorching droughts!

Your thorns are the camels of a time
When oases fled from the desert...

INCEPTION

My ancestor –
The Dolphin – conceived
Through the land of ice
And the test of fire…

Rowing the boat
Through the waters full of ice,
My selves sweated
More than when being near the flames…

My ancestor – the Dolphin
Swims slowly under a grizzled moon…

REFLECTIONS OF ALTER EGOS

To me you always remained obscure,
A trace of snow
Covering the heights no one ever climbed.

And I, like the moon,
Whitened with thoughts,
Keep hovering in the space filled with your light and shadow,
Failing to conquer any tower.

Until the end, the trace of snow remained
My reflection in the moony mirror…

PENINSULAS

I swiftly caught a bird on the shores of silence.

That rare singer refused to sing me any melody,
Be it the shortest one.

'Songs let out mute echoes
In the night's lonely islands,'
It said to me.

When darkness melts into sea glances,
And islands become peninsulas,
Deafness begins to sing a longing song.

Odyssey's Soliloquy

(Before arrival)

One day I will go back
To the place I never left from.
With my yes torn with horror,
I will watch you
That always mistook
The truth of returning
For the illusion of fleeing.

I never left for
Foreign lands.
Only my bones sailed through seas
Suddenly appearing on the horizon.

In fact, I never left my home…

THE PEEL

You say you disdain romantic affairs, my friend,
At a time that the cuckoo's song
Frightens you so much at winter nights,
Making you hide your dreams
From her echoes.

There are pincers that look like Stymphalian Birds.
That song, my darling,
Catches you, holds you tight
Like midnight dreams,
When misdoubts beat
Against the walls of curiosity,
As if they were bats.

Void of all romanticism, they beat and beat
Against your sparrow-like curiosity…

THE BAY

In his youth,
He would always return victorious from battle.

Every time he came back home,
Ships would anchor at the pier,
Longingly watching
The city they had left from.

Years have gone by.
With the growth of grizzle covering his head,
His victories have become scarce.

Now, after every loss,
He still dreams of the bay longingly,
Yet he nourishes a kind of feeling
That he would never reach there.

For, out of all battles,
Out of all despoliation and destruction of cities,
Even out of his then manly strength,
(Out of all things gone never to return),
Only the bays stood loyal to him...

MULBERRIES

To the little Hebrew children of my childhood

At Zachariah's home,
I ate mulberries,
Sweet mulberries
And baked fish with vegetables.

Then I angered at my mom
Who could never cook food
Like grandma Rachael did.

Many years have gone by since then,
But I – the child – still taste
That taste of sweetness
When I see generous believers
Feeding fish
Down there in the river near a temple…

The Guitar

How many guitars broke your silence?
Less than one?
More than two?
Silence itself was the breeze caressing the water sounds
That sprang up and died away in a dusky homeland.

How many guitars broke your silence?
How many guitars broke my silence?
Leaning against a fir-tree praising eternity,
I feel the owl's song piercing my bones.

How many guitars broke our silence,
Smelling oblivion
On every winter's eve?

To say nothing is much more difficult
Than to live with the sounds
That have abandoned both themselves and the seasons.

DEATH WAS NOT IN PARIS

"We must learn something from the trees."
              – Kasem Trebeshina

Death was not in Paris, my darling,
It had never walked
In Luxemburg's Garden either.

Every Autumn leaf
Was less than loneliness,
And the naked tree was quite unlike
The hesitating sounds of your guitar.

(Abandoned from whispers, it threw oblivion away –
Faint waltz cords
Filling the air of eternity.)

My sadness looked like the light at the verge of dusk:
That tree should have at least taught you
Why death was nowhere to be found in Paris.

You should have learned all only from the trees…

The Pilgrims' Tale

No one deigns
To listen to the tale from the very beginning.
Leaves are leaves,
And trees are trees.
Greenery always remains
A visual illusion,
Or an unconscious wooden bed.

I once love the fir that wasn't a fir,
Frightening solitude with azure branches.
Then, sleeplessness tired me so much
That I fell like light feather over tree crowns.

And right here starts the tale
Of what pilgrims said about me;
That I once was made up of flesh and blood,
But afterwards, one September night,
Becoming a wattle of leaves, I lost the sense
Of feeling the fervor of your body.

Cold like I was in the genes of my origin,
I breathe under candle shadows at nights,
Without understanding anything
From the fragile game of the tiny little flame.

… And the tale ends every moonlit night
When you, drunk with blinding bodies,
Pray to VENUSES wearing misty faces …

You are such a sad pilgrim
Travelling along roads of leafless trees …

Peaceful Mornings

Nothing could save you
Even love failed
To show you the path
To Tramuntana

Your freedom kept wandering in other spaces
And thus could never encounter anyone on horizons
(Even eagles saw it nowhere)

Nothing could save you
Even love failed
To tell you why Tramuntana winds blew

You saw only breathless birds on shoulders of storms
And thus you avoided meeting seagulls
In crystal clear skies

Nothing could save you
Even love failed
To teach you
The secret of blinking beams

You would always abandon peaceful mornings…

THAT PAINFUL EDGE OF LIGHT

(An imaginary dialogue with Garcia Lorca)

He had told me Granada Hills
Differ not a lot
From the hills of my birthplace
He had also told me
Winds have no homelands

'Perfumes – flowers – knives'
You once wrote
And I knew not that such a melody
Sprinkles guitar sounds at evenings

Even light has no homeland
I had told you
Dawn is dawn on all shores
And none has ever angered
At flowers

Perfumes and serenades and oranges
Your endless Andalusia, my darling
So I know not which orange
Shelters that painful edge of light
Or you might have picked it up
And now you dislike telling me the truth.

TOGETHER WITH THE SUN

One day will come together with the sun
To put an end to your migration through foreign lands
With the help of seagulls
And of fish that used to shine our nights
We will find our words gone with winds

So the first dawn, the second dawn
And the third dawn will return again
And our voices – my light –
Will echo through the dawns of all the seas of the world

Deep voices
Once lonely
Of which the only prelude
Is a guitar chord.

You, Wandering in Search of Light

O you wandering in search of light
Carrying a piece of sky on your broad shoulders,
Fill my evening of breaths and oblivions
With voices.

O you wandering with me at rhythm of waves
Lend me these fascinating infinities
Just for a moment.

I am like you
A human being still loving
And I have enough ears to listen to symphonies of shells
And I have enough eyes to see whispers
Of homeless winds of your migrations.

He that sees the sea but once
Parts with it as many times as winds do…

With No Sweat at All

Nothing is as precious as silence.

Flowers have bloomed even in wrong places.

Stones translated into water
With no sweat at al.

Flowers have bloomed even in wrong places.

Moses always lives
In the memory of His Stick.

Even flowers that failed to bloom will dry away…

A Delayed Chord

O little tiny butterfly, you tremble
Like a delayed chord on guitar strings.

O little tiny butterfly, night is silent,
An orphanage sheltering blind bats.

It keeps the sounds hovering,
It makes the words fall into silence,
It makes the song suffocate.

You tremble and tremble like a soul in wind.

A blooming tree at the edge of volcanic abysses…

A SONG

The swan lowers her neck
To touch the waters,
And translates into brightness...

The dawn snatches the song
From the bird's throat,
And translates into Night...

My Guitar, Wake Up

Unknown paths always bear flower names.
Horizon is the home of missed roads.
A guitar sound lies between one and the other.
Twilight, please teach me how to lament
For the vine dried with frost.
Sunsets dye in the redness of wines they never drank.
Grape berries bring greenery to our losses.

My guitar, wake up, wake up at dawn…

NOTHING BUT LIGHT

Nothing but light
And a single leaf at dusk
Can remind me of that of image of purity…

I loved you like love
I forgot you like childhood shells
Expecting that I would find them again there the other Saturday…

Nothing but light
Reminds me of those times
When the shells fled to other seasons
To other autumns
To other heavens
To sow the purity of my longings…

Dear lover, you first abandoned your own self
Then you turned your back to me and all the horizons
Never to turn into an image
Never to remain an infinite longing…

Nothing but light
Reminds me of your berserk parting
And I tremble like a leaf
Whenever my branches ache…

THIS SKY

This cloudy sky over Copenhagen
A sudden homeland of fleeing hieroglyphs
Will come back to my mind
Teaching you once again
That to speak of misunderstandings of languages, nations, races
Is but meaningless chattering
On the part of your father angering, for your son
Complains of nothing after a glass of beer
And can never match an invincible Viking...

This sky of hieroglyphs is as understandable
As your children's rhetoric about humanism
Addressing to men who never lived in peace
Not because they did not love peace, no
Not because they did not knew peace, no...

The only alphabet nobody taught us
(And unwillingly neglecting all kinds of rhetoric)
Is your deep eyes nailed in me
Though perhaps I knew not they had started a new journey...

And time elapses, and seasons do change
And moments fly away like piano sounds
Heard behind the fir-trees in a winter park
We celebrate our partings, our loves, our repentances and oblivions
Then we sing to the lack of presence for a while
With the sweetest words we had never chosen...

I love you as much as love itself
I love you with the craziness of the tree trunks dreaming to touch the sky

That just winks at them and leaves for another destination...

I love you beyond all the meanings that exhaust human race
How did it happen? Why did he come? Where did he go? Will he
come back?
Even if you are nowhere, you will be everywhere
Even if you always fail to come, you will never go away
From me or the skies or the season whose signs I know well

You, the newly created hieroglyph
Under a beautiful sky
And far from the earth where you are a passerby...

LIMIT

The woman watching the see is blind. For her, the sea waves are the soul waves. From now on, the chopped light of the immense water container is what she will see running deeper and deeper inside herself.

The blind woman and the ship that could never sail are of the same age. The ship and her last lover have the same farsightedness.

Her last lover was a sailor and a fool. He heard only the melody coming from the beating stick, turning a deaf to ear to all the island's playing drums.

The blind woman and her last lover loved the flute sounds at dusk.

He never told her that the sea light had the shape of his destroying love for her. However, she would willingly pretend that she had understood him. She feared that he might also go blind if she told him the truth.

Souls

Wounded seagulls
Wandering
About waters

The sky covering in sea sadness...

WHEN DEATH PILES UP

They should not have piled those dry branches up here
It is midday and the crowd
Will soon pass by them
The forest ghost will terrify the Dead
With the marrow dried in his bones
Then he will convey the crowd's death
Like an electrical conductor permits a flow of energy
They should have piled them up in the heart of the Bazaar square
But no, by no means
At midday

THE DEATH'S PAWS

Death has white paws
With the hare's soft fur
And blinding whiteness
Like that of the tiger's teeth

With the hare's soft fur
We rub ourselves
On meadows
Growing narcissi flowers
But the lake in the middle of them
Never shows us
The tiger's reflection...

The Lotus Eaters

We started the celebration party
With the golden calf on the table

We all spoke
The same language

After suffer
We forgot all what we had eaten

In the garden the first cock
Cracked dawn for the third time

BIRDS

Birds were flying inside the abandoned house
And around its yard's surrounding walls covered in thorny bushes reaching
    for the sky
No stick could draw water from stone
Though they said it was the rainy season

The Unreachable

Even at that dusk
The sun failed to reach the orange tree
And I remained with the essence of the fruit stuck to my fingers
While the sun continued to disappear into the horizon

The Water's Deaths

The water never passes away
Only glances do die
At the dawn of the day
A dawn is a dawn
For it quenches its hunger and thirst by becoming pregnant with
glances
And resurrects amidst the water's strange deaths...

His Widow

His widow will continue to live her earthly years under the shadow of the emperor's courtyard.

He, the most wonderful tree, left her soul empty with the crowds still conquered by him.

The crowds always look at his widow as a mantel of leaves.

When the blossoms wither, the mantel ceases to exist. At this moment even the crowds stop thinking.

In spring the mantel rejuvenates again. His widow gladdens because of the freshened memory of the citizens who never knew the dictator.

His widow loved the crowd and the leaf.

They both have short memory.

I Am a Non-Eu National

That beggar under a bridge of the River Sien
Crouching around the age of misery
With a bony dog beneath his feet
Thanks me for the donated Euro.
'It will buy me bread for tomorrow,' says he in English.

When I ask him where he is from, he answers that he is not a Parisian.
'Destiny brought me here by accident,'
'Someone whom I loved with all my soul,' splutters he, with hatred.
'But I am not from Eastern Europe,' adds he, with contempt,
'The place whose people pray to flee to Western World.'
(His looks at me with starving eyes).

'I know,' I say, 'I am a non-EU national, too.'
The beggar grins and says, 'It is impossible.'
'Yes,' I insist, 'I am from the Balkans,'
'And a woman named Mother Teresa,
'Blood like mine ran in Her veins.'

'I am a non-EU national,' I repeat, and he grins.
'It is impossible,' says he, stubbornly.
'People there are too poor to afford a plane ticket.'
'Those motherfuckers wonder about everywhere,'
'Those motherfuckers do all they can to get passports like ours.'
'They cost us too much, yes, too much.'

'They and the Syrians have filled the camps in my homeland,'
'They caused me to lose my welfare benefits
That I had been receiving from my government for 20 years.'

'Cursed be them! Cursed be them!'
'My welfare benefits helped me to travel.'
'I could freely fly from one airport to another.'
'Ah, those motherfuckers, one by one, had to go through checks.'

Thus chattered an EU beggar
To me, the traveler, the non-EU national...
His bony dog licking his feet.

Only Tulips...

The tulip twilight
And the silence of a stone in the forest
Always became my growth reaching for the unknown light...
The shinier the daylights
The more transparent would the sadness of seasons grow
Inside bones of flowers
And amidst sudden sounds blowing through trees
Had love hidden in strange shapes
Or had the turquoise tulip suddenly conceived itself
With light, stone and murmurs...?
My own self grows stalks and stands still...
Only a tulip that knows the other tulip
Can tell us the secret of blooming...

THIRST

She passed by the waters in a hurry without looking at them
Driven by the fear of missing the train
That never arrived at the station in time…

Her being became the homeland of thirst
Suddenly while she stood in the queue of passengers
Waiting to leave for the place she would not reach in due time…

Another traveler was waiting beyond a space
Equally drunk with eagerness and impatience
To see the woman who had passed by the waters
Without stopping for a while…

HE

He will not be able walk out of the house where he and the Eagle stay imprisoned.

He is there, and the guitar sounds coming from beyond the window, though tempting, fail to encourage him.

He and the Eagle love and hate each other infinitely.

She will not pluck his eyes out, for he has given up watching since his childhood. To both of them, light particles are as strange as colors.

She will not blind him, and he will cry one day, he will cry a lot because of her farewell.

At that moment he will be a child conscious of his loss, while the fir-trees will throw thick shadows over the sadness of the undiscovered oases.

DISTANCE

He is three hours away from the Swan's Neck.

The screams of the bird have been staying frozen on those shores since the midnight of the last song.

He is three nights away from the songs and a life away from the screams.

NOTE

"The Bay" first appeared in *FourW twentyfive Anthology*

"My Guitar, Wake Up" first appeared in *San Diego Poetry*

"This Sky" first appeared in *The Curlew*

"Only Tulips..." first appeared in *Michigan's Best Emerging Poets*

About the Author

Alisa Velaj was born in Albania, in 1982. She holds a Ph.D. in Albanian Language and Literature, which she has been teaching as subjects at university level, while writing poetry, prose, essays, articles, and research studies. Velaj was shortlisted for the annual international Erbacce-Press Poetry Award in UK in June 2014. Her work has been published in over 100 international online forums, printed magazines and anthologies across many countries (USA, UK, Sweden, Australia, Israel, India). Alisa earned an Artist-in-Residence Scholarship in February 2019 and attended the AIR Litteratur Västra Götaland Program in Villa Martinson, Jonsered, Sweden. In 2020, she won The National Prize in Poetry, awarded by the Albanian Ministry of Culture.

About the Translator

Ukë Zenel Buçpapaj is an Albanian writer who has published books of poetry and prose at home and abroad. His translation work has appeared in *Denver Quarterly* (USA, 1994); *Seneca Review* (USA, 1995); *Modern Poetry in Translation* (UK, 1996); *Visions International* (USA, 1996 and 1997); *The Year Book of American Poetry* (USA, 1997); *Grand Street* (USA, 998); *Fence* (USA, 1999) etc. He had also translated several great poets into Albanian. Among them, worth mentioning, are: Walt Whitman, Emily Dickinson, Robert Frost, Thomas Stearns Eliot, Ezra Pound, William Butler Yeats, Ana Ahmatova, Arthur Rimbaud, Octavio Paz, Seamus Heaney, Allen Ginsberg, Philip Larkin, John Ashbery, Mark Strand, Rita Dove, Lucille Clifton, Sylvia Plath, Wallace Stevens, Gerald Stern, Carolos Williams, E. E. Cummings, Robert Lowell, Yehuda Amichai, Ronny Someck, and Naim Araidi. He holds the following titles: 'International Visitor' (USA , 1992); 'Honorary Fellow in Creative Writing' (University of Iowa, USA, 1992) and 'Fulbright Scholar' (University of Iowa, USA, 1992).

A Professor Doctor, he is currently teaching Comparative Literature, Literary Translation, Contrastive Linguistics and Study Skills at the University.

www.ingramcontent.com/pod-product-compliance
Lightning Source LLC
Chambersburg PA
CBHW020215090426
42734CB00008B/1078